Surface Impressions

By Stephen Sandy

POEMS

Surface Impressions

Black Box

The Thread, New and Selected Poems

Thanksgiving over the Water

Man in the Open Air

Riding to Greylock

End of the Picaro

Roofs

Stresses in the Peaceable Kingdom

PROSE

*The Raveling of the Novel: Studies in
Romantic Fiction*

PLAYS

*Seven against Thebes: A Version of
Aeschylus' Tragedy*

*A Cloak for Hercules: A Version of
Seneca's "Hercules Oetaeus"*

Surface
Impressions

A POEM

Stephen Sandy

Louisiana State University Press

Baton Rouge   2002

Designer: Laura Roubique Gleason
Typeface: Sabon
Printer and binder: Thomson-Shore, Inc.

Library of Congress Cataloging-in-Publication Data:

Sandy, Stephen.
   Surface impressions : a poem / Stephen Sandy.
      p. cm.
   ISBN 0-8071-2762-0 (alk. paper) — ISBN 0-8071-2763-9 (Pbk. : alk. paper)
   I. Title.
   PS3569.A52 S87 2002
   811'.54—dc21

   2001005341

Some parts of this text have appeared in *Green Mountains Review* (second sec-
tion of "Barrens" as "Passages"); *Ploughshares* (first section of "Riding
Thermals" as "Heat Wave"); *Salamander* ("Parking Lot," "Triptych," "Lobster
Cove"); and (in different form) *Smartish Pace* ("Third Avenue," "Buzby
Afternoon").

I am grateful to the editors of those periodicals, to the Bellagio Study and
Conference Center, to the Corporation of Yaddo, and to the Lannan Foundation
and Provincetown Fine Arts Work Center for generous support during this book's
composition.

NATIONAL
ENDOWMENT
FOR THE ARTS

This publication is supported in part by a grant from the National
Endowment for the Arts.

CONTENTS

Surface Impressions

Parking Lot

Hard to believe the racket geese make, squabbling,
holding a confab in the dark—pitch dark to him
padding back to check the lights; yes, the windows
are dark.
          But that honking down on the pond, like angry
taxis, stops him: late geese on their way—he thinks—
homeward. But geese are home, wherever. A continent.
Are acting without accomplices; no past
or future to know. That squawky banter is
an irremediable thing.
                    He makes for his car, the office
shut down. Now someone passes him. They know each other—
each speaks with mild surprise the other's name,
no more. And heads his separate way across the dark.

1   BARRENS

1

Today to Herring Cove, my beach hat blew
downwind, I didn't even notice—four-foot seas,
that roar of light. "It's more than water," the boy said
when first he saw the ocean at Ogunquit,

you go into trance, a doze, a mental place
with nothing on-screen, till the rays, working under
the wind-rub, as if an appraising look grazing
your flanks, press lightly like a meaning hand.

A child, whole and looking on, who was about
to have his tonsils out lay out on a white
sheet, his mother's hand in his when a nurse
gave him a balloon and smiled, saying, "now

blow this up." The brown membrane went taut,
harder to inflate than red ones at parties. He watched
amazed, the sphere before his eyes grew large
as he sank back—grip loosened—mother gone,

it was sailing him off, clearest white gulps like this
onshore wind filling lungs with ozone-laden air,
an engine rumbling out there, low breathings as I sink
into lights above the dark; then joy, then nothing.

When I came here, in the room on the white sink
on the enamel that shone in the sun, an ant lay,
a large one on its back with legs curled, perhaps
a carpenter ant, alone, undone by something,

forgotten by the cleaning person who swept up
before I came. Why did I leave it there?
What am I hoping for? What that black mark
on the white could mean for me: I did not decide

to leave it. I did not neglect it. I didn't think
about it but observed it when I was doing up
the dishes. Today it's moved to the other
edge. Was it the wind? A moment of life?

I walk down to water's edge, the wet stretch below
the hem of weed and tide trash, from the beginning
a part forever (still) public—"not any" owns it
Thoreau relates, as the Indians told *the committee*

from Plymouth of the cape north of Eastham.
"'Then,' said the committee, 'that land is ours.'"
Now then: it's mine, walking the free margin,
here & there dotted by bottle cap, Styrofoam bit;

no shell or spar or glass, no bathers in the brine;
up beach, a crowd of singles baste for broiling.
I thought to claim a spot and find one, but feel
vibes; small, meaning looks from the women near.

I hold my sand—that is, for two minutes, when I
look again and see breasts, brazen.
       Back
at the old spot, my hat: I thought what a miracle
it hadn't flown until I saw the sand put in it

≈

by some protective hand: "this must be my hat,"
I advised the pair that had assumed my sand:
they paid no mind, oiling their thighs and chests.
Stillness, there on the threadbare prayer rug of sand.

Take this Miter, a thing of stillness, tawny cone
dappled with orderly orange spots, a boon
from the sea spiraling up to its tip then into space
spiraling on; but it comes from Melanesia

and commerce brought it to Commercial Street,
where art brought me. Behind the wheel, where I
had cleaned my dashboard at last, the *idiot light*
gleamed red in sunlight. Nothing wrong, the light

≈

was off, just bright as a shell wet from the sea,
yet worrying, chafing me. But I do, after
a certain point, lose point, edge; go off,
forget the point maybe, the point of a shell's

spiral nipped in the crash of a tide, find
it all gives pause, or might ("you're fine, the swim team's
ready to go, still in the water; perhaps
you should look into it") such as ascertaining

where ramps begin, where steps, low risers then high,
on the medieval lanes of P-town. The legend
under the light (not on but ready) reads
MAINTENANCE REQUIRED. Tell me about it! Where

are rest rooms, did I take the Zocor, look at the map—
I am not like that woman's labs trained
to piss at tide line while she stands by proudly.
I check location of the bathhouse before I sit

by all that falling water. (One at Town Hall;
one, not on the map, down in Merchants Hall,
good to have spotted.) An older overweight man,
pendulous breasts (what happens pumping iron

perhaps long after, but it happens, when
the free weight of fate bears down), wearing
black briefs, starts his corgis; they're off
jogging the beach. Gratitude for this minor

glamor, the light, the up-volume as breakers fall;
no boom box, no vocal, thank you for that, Lord.
Here, the leopard skin of the Measled Cowrie
ground down to purple glassy skin and the Lord's

Prayer (would it be superfluous to say,
superfluously?) engraved on it. Whose
perfect story, imperfect alibi? That's
a hell of a note, that blindness. Here the cheapest

souvenirs Commercial Street can tender
are shells, shells with nothing to say, no logos
(till we start engraving), though one might sing, "now
voyager, buy me for your windowsill,

though I am mean and poor and one of millions."
That tropic Cowrie and fifty like it in a tub
were sure in dutch with the Almighty, I guess,
until some careless entrepreneur with crew

of hungry boys gathered them, corrected
"the very dangerous error" of being silent,
wordless and beautiful at once.
                                        So what am I
doing on this shore, nothing but tossing waters

between me and Europe? Thinking of something else.
People are friendly, if minding their tourist business
with a smile is friendly, tolerant at least, but none
is one of those I love, from whom the intervention

of 300 miles is helping me to value, miss,
account for. It's the space for a time between that makes,
let's say, the heart go yonder. Whatever this is.
A passion mixed of need and habit? The feeling

of *at home,* as when you are known, personally,
to an animal, preferably a pet and one you chose,
not one that chose you like a barn cat with feral
pinings, but with designs on your hearth rug too;

poor mutts the pound missed, or the unkillable
woodchuck sapping your foundation. What
I hear in my mind's ear is church bells, I
don't mean wedding chimes but rather *something*

⌒

understood. My screen saver shows a tropic sea,
jellyfish flouncing, sea horse trotting, flounder
idling, fabulous tropicals, shells on the sand
bottom; out the window above the screen

growls no virtual deep but Melville's ocean,
the whale's path, sea of origin, of return. Today
I watched for sea strife at Race Point, no kelp
or shell tossed up; one tiny silver fish,

a glinting eye stared; not imploring, blind
or stupefied, to find me of this ether element.
It's one world, as Wendell Wilkie would say,
and I can go to The Shell Shoppe for a Megpie—

⌒

if I fancy the Philippines. No fishermen left
in this fishing port, save one or two for show
out on Macmillan Wharf for summer people.

Gray, middle-aged men in motorized wheelchairs
join the mob that throngs Commercial Street
on Labor Day. I don't know what it means,

I'm making nothing up as I go along,
feel this intensely and as intensely feel
I must not try to find for it the shape

it's capable of taking on, the way
water charging ahead into oblivion
will say OK, become cubes if you freeze it,

and which would take away that flea market
miscellaneousness and glut of trivia,
the awful random clutter of deserved oblivion
that pulls you in and says, *this here is it.*

This here begins to bring up something else.
But that's all right, especially if we see it
from the viewpoint of a small-scale society,
which we may well become, some version of one,

this global shopping spree we're getting to be;
an effect unplanned-for the way Thoreau, by the time
he got around to *Cape Cod,* sounds like many
a Victorian book of rambles, save for a few

high points outbursts of angry grieving soul

enraged with insight—for the moment. Shall I

show you something from my baggage? The scar

where the titanium plate was taken out

four years after a mugger broke my arm

with a baseball bat? My apologies to the fucker,

I didn't have the money he so fiercely needed.

Or the astrolabe compass I brought here,

these days a mariner's joke, a paperweight,

but a reminder (date, 1914) too,

medieval instrument that British officers

carried at the hip into battle in that forgotten

war, half modern half Homeric.
                              I'm taking
them as they come, these thoughts like skipping stones
that trip along the water till they fizzle,
sinking.
                Then one day the phone rings; ———

your dear friend has cancer and you see,
not much wiggle room there, is there?
                                During
a walk in the dune lands thinking about ———,
I climb the mophead hillocks, tossing sand-waves

cresting—freeze-frame slow-mo—wind-shaped pitch pine,
blueberry, dune grass, holly, beach goldenrod,
                —sky blue, sand yellow, pine green—primary hues,
primal place, no movement here but gulls,

sprays of rose hips like molten ingots, piecemeal

bicyclers and a few impeccably buff
people taking their bronze physiques for a walk,
this spit of land so small it will hardly hold

an A&P let alone a Wal-Mart, was never
intended, if there be intention, intention
aloft or under, to be inhabited by us

—that is, citizen consumers, rather than mice
or voles or sand snakes, these lands that no people
QUOTE own QUOTE but jam up in like a crowd

on Saturday night in some back room of the spirit,
the orderly, spotless desecrations of the land
where no one builds or flies in from Boston,

such anyway human scale, the bike paths, board-
walks, roses, trim shrubs, like a gardener's version
of the Sahara.
           The gent who runs the Visitor
Center bookstore piles his stock of *Cape Cod*
by the register, but he is outside, smoking.

Soon then the wind; beyond the final dunes
the sea, and children screaming as the sea
fondles them with a falling *shush,* one frothy
touching when a wave, nonchalant, reaches
in and withdraws. Sand stings the brow—but here

among bright flowers.
           Police siren ("zero tolerance")
back there. But only among these stillnesses.

2

A dozen times more tempting to wash up—
the sink of supper, snack, breakfast dishes—
than to do your sit-ups and sit up and face
the blank page of day, the day's blank page.

But it isn't empty, the white paper, I
know that; like a fading dream, we must coax
the innards out and get 'em down on paper
or what was there in a surround of clarity

on waking will fade into the bestial (or
at any rate, quotidian) sidebars of
the mail, the dishes, sounds of workmen, thoughts
of others, the whole long blessed day.

One year, finding myself in the right countryside
or ending up there like Keats on his walking tour
I would meet the poet I admired so much
and called. And called. At length the man answered,

asked me to Pine Spring for a beer. Following
directions, I found his upland place, a farmhouse
and barns in a glade of pine and cedar. No one there.
I called, walking in the sunlight and shade. At last

a child of five or so sauntered around
the corner of a shed. He seemed worried yet
polite. I asked him where his father was.
—Granddad? He's in the garden. —Where, I wondered,

was the garden? —Just up that road, the boy
waved toward a track and disappeared into
the house. Up this path a quarter mile and more
where nothing grew that one would call a garden

I trekked: mullein and milkweed, chicory, wild carrot,
the sort of growth that edges in when a road
gets left unused for long enough. I was
beginning to wonder. What garden had the boy in mind?

Maybe he shared the same retirement from the world
his grandfather was called a recluse for.
I thought of Li Bai's poem "On Visiting
a Taoist Master in the Mountains," when

the visitor arrives he finds no one; he listens

to the trees in light above, a waterfall
and a dog's bark in the distance; learns his lesson.

But here I was, and *it* was. A garden fenced
with wire to discourage deer, orderly rows

of cabbage, onion, lettuce, corn, tomatoes.
No one in sight. I called out to him, *Master!*

The garden glistered in the sun. He was so
private he was not even there. "That man

has many trip wires, a lot of 'em," a mutual friend
had said. He desired not privacy

but isolation. I was invasive, I presumed—

and shivered.
                    A voice from the garden spoke my name.
I answered that I was there. He said, come in

and close the gate; I'm over here. He was down
behind the corn. He said, I've got to finish

these two rows. I dropped on hands and knees,
no stranger to weeding. *Hoe,* I thought; *hoe corn.*

No word from the poet. Twenty minutes later,
we've done. We stood. Wordlessly closed the gate.

I followed down hill. He opened beers. The child
was gone. We sat in shade. At last he spoke.

—Nothing makes a difference. I'm glad you came.
Why do you want to be a poet? —Because I am,

it's what I've always done, I said. —You're wrong,
he said. You'd not *be* here if that was all
you did. You're down there in that awful program.
I said, how nice the place he had here was.

Strange, but now he shifted; wandered. —It's all
I have, I can't afford to keep it; town
is ruined anyway. The greedy think
they can become developers by putting up

a trailer park. I'll have to leave. You, too!
Poetry makes nothing happen, like the fella said.
Hah! Remember, thunder. It'll come. Just wait.
I'll show you my work shed, then you can go.

                                               It was neat,

a milk house or the like, but cold in winter, not

an elegant hut such as the fond retreats

in Chinese "mountain-water" paintings, but then

I thought they, too, must freeze in winter; boy

with a hand-warmer at the ready, snow outside.

—Want you to know something. I'm not alone here.

We take walks, my father, father's spirit, me;

my daughter—she's in town shopping. But still

I'll have to sell this place and find a job.

       I saw it was time I left, he'd be glad of that.

—Keep in touch; *by letter,* he cautioned, leaning into

my car. —Write, keep writing. I'll write back.

3

. . . Now e-mail tells John's troubles up in Brimfield,
water rises dead-leaf brown from the new well.
Somehow those beavers tapped into his water supply.

Nothing to drink? Bottled H_2O in gallon jugs
will do till you get it fixed—but eschew those little
designer *bouteilles:* today I ordered a gardenburger

—and water. "No water," unless I pay $1.79
for a three-swig flask. "We don't have any water," she says.
Out here, the bay's in sun, aflame with gold ahead,

hammered silver right and left; motionless
cumuli aloft. Low tide, I walk where sea will be:
unmoving lucent pebbles in clear water.

Now Willy off to the whale-watch boat with his lady,
short-sleeved shirt and a khaki army vest, *my he
going to shiver,* getting a little gray on top,
but I recognized him this morning sitting in the sun

heavy into his Walkman; haven't laid an eye on him
thirty years but there's that shapeliness of skull
comes back, right off, never forget a face or
the bones under it, maybe the way you can't forget

riding a bike—though god knows they've changed bikes—
or the leather-face geezer once a flower child and his
rheumy guitar singing the Beatles for tips in front of
Town Hall I see that I saw now twenty years ago; then

＊

down street a man with a fifty-inch waist says to
a woman with sixty, *forty minutes to the boat.* This
crowd thins after Labor Day (but ratchets up in girth);
farther, beyond the billowing tummies, an Asian

bodybuilder strolls—or steps—in cutoffs, his lats
make arms hang out, pneumatically full pecs high
like hooters, his brown auto-sculpture marred
by alarming kyphosis, making torso

look like an art deco statue; who ever saw
anything like it? Not to say we aren't all beautiful
yet wasp-waist swivel gives a visual aid to mark
the pale whale-bodies of his matrix. Last week

＊

a whale-watch hit a right whale, rare beast these days,
collided prow on skull, with the animal it sailed (failed?)
to see, *protected* not *endangered* species. In Brimfield,
forget the whale, it's beaver, protected animal.

Watch the valley by the low streams overrun
with beavers we may not kill; weekends, citizens
of Brookfield Road in Brimfield (don't the old names
—not to speak of the cattails—give a hint as to

proximity of marsh, the colonial lay
of the land?) police their wetlands with spade and glaive
surreptitiously undoing what beavers did
weeklong, their dams creating reservoirs upstream

that fill the cellars of a working town. Their trouble is
not nature but innocent ecologists
adrift in their green thoughts of a green shade
that never was on sea or land: the beaver

was "extirpated" in New England—as naturalists know
and tell—three hundred years ago: by market forces,
trappers out for pelts to send to Europe for
the robes of merchant princes. In harsher words

these beavers were defunct until folks meaning well
but blind passed laws and plunked some beaver
by a Berkshire pond two dozen years ago. How soon
they multiplied and clogged the wetlands and our cellars!

But on the Cape, it's whales. The whales surface
to be enjoyed or to enjoy just tagging along
or playing tag—just bumping into humans, *hello*—
in the whale-path spouting greetings like the parrot

at the curb on Commercial Street who stops a crowd,
while somewhere in Maya country or out at sea
animals are trapped for cage or can, our appetites.
So we must bless them—part of nature part of us—

of *us*—they're at our doors, like the stoneware beavers-
at-the-ready on tiles announcing Astor the fur king's
Astor Place in the New York subway. The planet
will be fine just fine, *selah!* when we move on.

Shell Game

At The Shell Shoppe polished Trochi come half the size
of one my grandmother would show—"don't touch"—
nesting the nacre coil in her hands, hands
that proffered also their faintest aroma of banana oil.
Stationed on the sideboard, her pyramidal spiral
would gleam in sunlight that cut-glass tiebacks rainbowed
through the dining room from glazed French doors.

Here, minor

trophies, piddly Miters from the Coral Sea,
leopard spots once scarlet, faded to umber.
"There won't be more," the owner brags. Next door,
a jeweler: "harvesting shells like hers will get you
arrested, stateside. They're all from the Philippines."

2 MY MADAGASCAR

I

The sun of getting used to things is beaming light
upon our way, we who are left behind
and she, who was every part of us, off there.

She writes about her "first host family."
Hello? I'm not sure her first host family
wasn't this one, ours, her own. My guess,

we're only hosting them, these young we call
"ours," and any child's a foster child
at last. By definition, not your child

when she moves along, not yours, nor anyone's?
The "first host family" hurrahed to see her work.
"They thought I had servants where I came from."

Sunlight bloomed at the wooden eave, the weathered
pediment. Mosquito netting edged with beads
veiled the halls. No power, only those lamps,

candles in shallow cups. She sat watching
the garden air, winnowed by bats, the faint
warbles of paradisal birds, till morning.

What fear I did not know, I know now, and
murmurs on the air still inarticulate in me.
I see her ready, zoned for this and the embrace

of being on her own. Holding tight to the cloud
of what must be done, it's clear she has it now,
this thing, if she can learn to know the owl's song.

When poetry does not come as easily as leaves
to the trees, like the man says . . . O what is this—
now hear the critic mouthing about a work

that proceeds at life's pace rather than literature's?
This talking with her is hard enough, well, like
pulling quills, or digging nettles from the garden,

things unsayable or maybe only hard to say,
all tiny needles, not worth saying couched
as "waves of the flesh crashing against the shores

of spirit," or the like. Besides, I cannot
begin to know the weather of her mind,
season of heart, better than I can estimate

seasons of Madagascar, drought, dogmatic
heat such as, so far this side of the equator,
we never know; gruesome noontide of endless

dog days—but in January, seasons reversed—
one hundred ten degrees in the shade and all
the unfamiliar flowers, a thing like bush clover

but not; or pink axwort, but not; like vetch,
like chicory, asphodel, all of it wilting
and there in the shade of rattan awning—air

smelling of fish and bee balm, a blanketing chord,
monarda, needles-and-musk, eyes of the catch
shining, laid out, fuming far from its element.

My theme here, absence: reports of my absence
have been slighted—*shaken off as dewdrops
from the lion's mane.* My Madagascar

never got off the ground; would never happen.
From here on, his life in Madagascar would
be posthumous, life among symphonia trees,

screw pines, among the golden palms, they're golden
but sharp on the shins, read about it in
his obit, the one in NATURAL HISTORY. The man

would fall off the edge, as the Spanish pundits said
Columbus would if he sailed too far, at least
it felt that way, coasting aimlessly through

clouds, little colonies of Malagasy, shoals
of folks wearing gold rings and medals flashing
in sun from breaks in the white; cruising along

under his celluloid parachute. He never shook
on anything! Softly, old boy, softly. *Hello
is anyone home,* he calls as he lands and opens

the door and treads the stairs of his life, his narrative
flow. Poets make nothing happen? Lucky folks!
The songs you hear are the ditties sirens sing

from archipelagos of absence, distant
as the whale-like wail of lemurs, the loud cries
of lemurs calling lemurs miles away.

Tents on wooden platforms, German campers
loud in the forest with their solar power, their
bratwurst and onions sizzling below the bats

and swallows circling above Kirindy—Germans,
pouring their mountains of M&M's from satchels.
This may be sequestered as any corner of the globe,

but where electric generators clang, high tech's
not far behind. What insect—is that a cricket,
a cicada?—lacks its aria, gig to punctuate

your stillness? Loud as hell, those indri lemurs
yowl and wail in the trees. A tree frog throbs.
A lizard skitters, weaves dry leaves at your feet.

But these must be your words not mine. That simple!
I can't imagine where you are because
I am not there. Madagascar gets to be

a state of mind; my state. "That slope may look
insignificant but it's going to be our destiny,"
Klaus Kinski said last night in an old movie,

at a tributary's bend swarming with flies,
rubber-mad heart of darkness on the Amazon—
not my words; but I thought of us as trying

to forge ahead upstream just far enough
to strike it rich for us both. Anyone who says
he's never felt the need to strike it rich

is talking through his hat, the one with the wide
false modesty brim. Well I know how you feel,
I know what you're saying, Mr. Longbeard in T-shirt

at the convenience counter shelling out for gas
and ten bucks more for dollar tickets, SUNNY SIDE,
FAT CHANCE, MILLION DOLLAR SMILE, and more—*this*

one here, yes that one there, just tear off one
of each; while outside tires of our waiting wheels
enjoy the chance of flattening because some previous

customers were breaking bottles on the pavement
by the pumps—frustrated by something, you might say.
"It's a lot steeper than I thought," Fitz said

when he saw the mountain he had to level to get
his steamboat over the isthmus. We do what we

have to do, do it, stop, give out; or in.
Giving like that happens. At first the tube

is fat and full; you squeeze it, you roll it up
then, *pooft.* Chuck it. We work on what we have

and then "we need some Italian opera very much."
Everyone waiting it out, asleep or not asleep.

Footsteps on dry grass, and sand; voices; starlight.
Do not ask questions, it will not work. The rumpled

coats we wear, part of the deal. Play that hand
of trinkets you were dealt close to the chest.

2

Wanting to live life "deliberately" as Thoreau
averred when he took to Emerson's real estate
for a spot of exile—borrowed that woodlot with cunning
to write his sermons from solitude; she flew

to the red rocks, limestone needles of Bemaraha,
to the cut woodland where only baobab trees
remain, prince of her Antipodes, that other end
of earth, daughter taken below by twin desires—

for knowledge, risk, taken below for years
to Antananarivo, to Morondava, at last
to tiny Andranomena—goats and geckos,
chickens, tin-roof shack her cottage now,

slapped with fresh coats of turps, the roach-queller
varnish, just for her. Who was it made her go
to the isle at the bottom of the world? He called
in the strange tongue, subtropic heat: come forth

from the cave, the head desk clerk when the phone rang
from worlds away, the Tana' Hilton lobby
(size of a two-car garage) a lobby babble
backdrop of every phrase, each phrase I say

echoing as I say it, boomeranging off
our satellite out there . . . somewhere! Did you hurt
did you —hurt your knee badly? Badly?
                                        —"It's nothing—ing
but O the street kids—ids, out from their tin-can hovels!"

"Has anything happened—appened—in the world?"
she asks down there as if from the bottom of a cistern.
"Is no news—news—just no news?"
                                        The Serbs,
I begin, and Kosovars . . . "But has anything

happened near you I—ear you I
should know? —know?"
                                        Whatever it is submerged
she wants to surface, I am not sure, I hope
this confab lightens up, I tell her no

nothing, nothing's happened, but the cat blew lunch—
yes lunch . . . half a mouse. Epiphanies and empty
boats! Bane and blessing. Is this pain
or pleasure? She sounds certain—and nervous, anxious

to serve, that great blank where will and charity
meet, helpless without an object, a world
to be described when that is all there is
to be done, a people to be inscribed on a self;

play the earned disjunctions out, mount risk;
get arms around the good stuff and the bad together.

    "No dysentery—and oh! I love you!"
                                        Voice
unequalizes, no longer there; background

fades out. I set the white receiver down;
it fits there, snug in its cradle. Tears, idle tears,
I know just what they mean.
                                —Shortest verse,
the man said, in the King James version. "He wept."

3

Dear daughter, let me tell you how things are here.
First, rain. What happened to those thermal patterns
we grew up with? Rain, every day. "The crops

are rotting in the valleys" of upstate New York, the walls
are leaking like the roofs. Then heat. Last night
I drove to the Performing Arts Center, muggy dell,

Lowell was playing the piano in Bach's *Musical
Offering for Violin Flute Piano*—well, also
to hear the Beethoven Boulez and Berio (evening

of the four B's), the concert excellent, a peach
melba for the ear but especially what Bach made
of a fugue, a tune crafted by his patron,

Frederick the Great, to test Bach's mettle. But first
I found myself at the wrong entrance where
ten thousand youths were getting wired for the stars,

their rock band, while the warm-up rumbled within,
a distant thunder. They knocked back Seven-Up
anchored with vodka, blew fogs of smoke, then chucked

green bottles in the bushes, meaty youths
stripping off T-shirts while they showed their tickets;
a voice from hidden speakers in the trees announced

the next concert, Counting Crows—yeah, sure—
no beverages allowed, shirts optional, mosquitoes
certain, West Nile virus not in the picture.

They were heading over the bridge above a deep
romantic chasm that kept gate-crashers out,
down into the sunken amphitheater, a bowl

engulfed by humid August, like some Albert Hall
under the sea, a fin-de-siècle Ring Cycle
Wagnerian set now crammed with kids, twilight

adhering to tawny backs. Somewhere backstage
in fluorescent-bright greenrooms the stars will be
hanging out and thinking about the house. But I

am lost and have to go round the other side
for the little theater with classical music—drive out
past two lone troopers on horseback, around three blocks,

and there I am—stopped at a state police checkpoint.
A flat-brimmed hat leans in, *Have you been drinking?*
In this weather? Sure all day. No officer. Look here

sir you are not wearing a seat belt do you have
a medical reason for not wearing a seatbelt?
I only came around the block . . . only trying

to get to the chamber concert before it starts. . . .
It certainly is a privilege to sit in small
air-cooled theaters with no mosquitoes, good

acoustics, Bach, a Beethoven quartet. (This last
"in its way, a perfect piece," Ned reckons, pro
listener beside me in the seventh row.)

I'm not sure why the king's "test of the fugue"
moves me, perhaps because that dated illness *fugue*
comes to mind, ambulatory automatism

in which some hapless shop clerk would set off
on a journey without goal and which on his
return he could remember nothing of,

a Quest turned inside out, sad fellow compelled
to go for the gold—but no rainbow and no
pot at the end of it. *Insane travel,* or what

was once called wanderlust; seeing the world.
Is that what we have done . . . ? Surely you wouldn't
change your seaside hovel in Andranomena

for that Dionysian shock of rock even if
they had Bob Dylan. People with nothing to do
especially the young make up some things they really

have to do. But don't I do that too? Perhaps a cool
evening of Bach, Beethoven, Berio would suit you
for a change. You don't have enough change down there!

Nor me up here. I'm leashed to highbrow culture or
what passes for it and we hear that all that stuff
no longer matters. The house for Bach was a handful

compared to the drove of fans across the chasm.
At least they're out in the weather, as you are, it's only
us, out for art in the high old sense, who're cooled.

⌒

At a flea market, a spinster headed for sheltered care
had a bust of Shakespeare marked ten dollars, "take it
for six"; the bard in Beau Brummel coat looked proper,

well-off. She'd no idea who it was; had been her mother's,
the sight of it one of her earliest memories; then
in a blip from the collective unconscious, she blurted

"Shakespeare, it's Shakespeare"—pale chalk glowing in lamplight
like the marble it imitated. Some Malagasy
may know Shakespeare—a play, a face—better

than natives of these hills upstate. How to get on
without those things that make a life worth living?
What milk does one drink? What bread does one eat?

⌒

Well . . . after the daily douse of showers, it's clearing.
Last evening two foxes busy snuffing the turf
for grubs, too busy to check me out—standing there

bug-circled, amazed at the closeness—at last found time
to look—as if idly turning to be photographed—
holding their ground with that *look-at-my-*

to-die-for-bush expression, foxy smile: *you are
the errant one*—until with measured pace
they trotted into their ample twilit shade

of covert. This morning, a welt on my arm I don't
know what left there. But in the heat I feel
a snooze coming on. Estivation T. Cornpone

they call him. Love. . . .

4

We talk of visiting our daughter in Madagascar
which in any case is farther off than anyone
should want to venture. End of the earth, it costs

too much for two, the French having made this former
colony the costliest place on planet Earth
to get to. So who should go? She has a friend

in Athens. We could meet half way. . . .
                            It's hard to get past
Maya Angelou cooing about the lemurs—
voice-over for a documentary we watched;

I know I'd rather see my daughter than all that
psychedelic fauna, sci-fi Jurassic Park
of lost species, fantasia flora. But Athens . . .

Rain, it starts to splatter on North Main Street,
and I was only walking to mail your letter
to Madagascar (yours now, not mine)! Hot spot

and dry as a fly's breath on a scorching griddle;
cocoon-shaped Madagascar, exotic garden,
her Eden eddy in earth's strong currents. Has she

listened to the waves, that song, old chorus of
necessities? Amber region, fragile shell,
might turn and look over its own shoulder,

sea scarp, crenellate waste of waters. Will she
behold the lapse, the sands, dunes haunted by
continents like thunderheads on the horizon!

As a triton from the waves turned now to stone
lips pursed at his horn the conch he blows alone
amid sea spray, a silence, Indian solitude.

How long in the ocean's chrysalis can your shore
keep isolate of mauled Tanzania's blood,
immoderate refuge! Menagerie of lives,

those gridlocked generations, lidded eye,
green claw, red trill of the Fody bird, awkward
sifaka lemurs who have forgotten crawling

and amble, bouncing like stately kangaroos
or as if they copied Monty Python's man,
ancient Edwardian butlers on Benzedrine!

After the zebras have thundered over the hill
stillness resumes its profile like a pop-up umbrella,
villagers go about their usual chores, low sounds—

raking the rutted gravel among the huts,
winnowing rice, weaving wide-brimmed straw hats—
when someone with fresh batteries at the end of

the compound turns up the French station; people
slowly, first one then another, join in the song
from the radio soon silent, humming it or idly

singing along the village, a daylong communal
music, passing it back and forth knitting
the raveled silence, the lyric shared as a carol.

Undulant isobars of heat, rattan verandah
shades you from eyes, the indolent walking-near
of the women from washing, and the caw, always

the caw of blue sky, a rubbed blur on the dull
blackboard of sound where each shrill or articulate
voice is erased. And now the *Bureau de Poste*

mistress turns, nodding at noon, her cup beside
her plaiting, the tin roof; ample bosom rising,
subsiding; she dozes off as her sheets of imperforate

timbres-poste curl in the drawer, brown gum
of elliptical spindling sheets. Across the way,
universe of seashells, raffia hovels, eggshells.

Simian

*A sense of belonging among the dangers of
arrogance was what he needed, and he finds it*

*in others' ruling passions, those little parcels
of* joie de vivre *he gets to tour with by following*

*voices from the grave—guardian voice-overs you might say—
to walk him through the chickeny days. Quick*

*and dead, a double heritage, tapestry with front
kempt as a Kentish lawn, out back a squalor of loose*

*ends, the sheer draw of dust pouring from bins
of shadows. He has to live up to what he fears*

*most, din of mind, then live it down like a monkey
fallen asleep in the happy leafage of his tree.*

3   BEECH FOREST

Light from the ugliest lamp I ever saw, here
on the table that triples for reading, eating (can't say
dining), business on the phone; ugliest except
a few around the corner in that guest house at windows

—plaster driftwood; cylinders like rockets or sanitary
napkins propping shades; thin torso of a youth;
red globe on orange globe, the works, *somebody's*
collection. Wouldn't she love this one, lump of lamp base

intending landscape, two donkeys in mustard glaze,
heads ruefully down, one carrying two rush panniers
large enough to hold your pens or salts and peppers; on
the other a shifty man with droopy moustache rides,

grumping under his sombrero; right leg broken
off at the knee, left leg clipped at ankle. They make
no progress, this mold-made work—the joins, arthritic
ridges where dabs of grayish green suggest

a wizened bush from which a brass post rises
to hold a shade that doesn't fit and twice
has tried to burn, as crusty sores at the rim show.
Still, it lights my work. Why hate it? Do I care?

These indecorous furnishings stand for failure, are
a clutter that weighs down, defeats the purpose,
like dumbbells taken along on vacations; the pen jar;
lamp base, sextant, portable folding triptych.

The writing table fills with clutter. Specials
coax me to nudge buying into play. A checkout
coupon lets me get some brand of lunch meats
fifty-five cents off if I spend two dollars

but I just can't find it when I'm shopping, the ticket—
with its rubric of good news and inscrutable forest
of bar code, black on red—to lead me on; back home
there it is, on the table, laying waste my power to spend.

What I have wanted (with Larkin) to do must be
"essentially undoable, it belongs to the imagination."
Rather, the demolition has begun, piss and shit
and blood mix in the snow-white bowl; and yet

I find the Beech Forest (behind the beach
dunes) that Allen recommended "without
reservation." The man was right—it more
than satisfies, these beech ponds and their dune

forest. I sat on a pitch pine that had blown
over and then turned round and risen again,
the bowed part making a seat something like
a saddle; the tree was growing while I sat on it

as were the other pitch pines round the pond ruddy
in afternoon, late light of day, rough trunks
with tufts of twisted branches green with needles,
it was *idyllic,* wind speaking through the pines,

＊

solitude:—O, yes, two high-breasted girls
came striding by, I heard them coming, I
heard them going, yammering at full volume
not looking left or right, they passed me, were

out of sight and soon of earshot, Doppler effect
caused by exuberant youth in oblivious chitchat.
And people are smoking in these dry woods too,
not policing their butts is how I know,

the butts *will* surface from the heavier, sifting sand,
sand spilling, surfing down hills, crashing in waves
over the path here. But call it solitude,
when a thought—but wait! I thought—I should not be

＊

having a thought here, this moment: yet a vision
of a Chinese poet in his study overlooking
such a pond as this arrives out of the silence
like the yellow water lilies on the water, pads

spreading out in files like a design in the broadloom
of a lobby. The sage is working on a poem, brushing it
on silk, inspired by a blend of Tao and
Confucius. Doubtless he would not forget

allusions to Sung poets, if he were not
a Sung poet himself, in which case he would have to
echo Han or T'ang; and he would be writing
of solitude; time passing; absent friends

(enlightenment would have to be inferred).
No matter, I didn't bring a pen today.
However, over there are inkberry bushes, so
with a reed I just might make a start. . . . Farther

on the path I listen to a bird, a warbler perhaps,
I do not know the song or see the bird.
There with the pines and sand and birdsong, and no
prayer- or guide- or selfhelp-book, no

serious commune, the mind must yearn to be
led on; it wants a deity, an altar to approach;
an altar at least to take steps toward; occasion
to rise to—with nothing planned for the mind,

it's like a person suddenly blind, not blind
for a long time and knowing the ropes, but just
now, rope-stung, blind—and groping, feeling around
for the way, any way, or, closer to home,

when the power goes at night just getting from
here to there even though you know the drill,
—you never find the batteries when you need them,
groping down cellar for the circuit breaker then

you flip it; nothing, it's a bigger failure you are part of—
know the layout in general yet without ceremony
the mind leans forward, over an edge, hoping for,
needing a little ritual, like a guide rail to keep it

from falling, going down. Even then the mind
finds need of other news, keeps on desiring
alterity somewhere at hand. For example,
walking the streets of Provincetown, nothing to see

but lots to look at, all that fluff and buff,
the Michelin-man day-trippers aching along;
suddenly I want a prayer book, maybe not
Bottles and Stools or *The Little Red Book* but still . . .

even a pocket copy of *A Shropshire Lad,*
such as I find soon after all the buff and fluff
at Tim's, the only bookstore on the street,
handy for quick reads. Thin as a shortbread biscuit,

THE RICHARDS PRESS LONDON 1915, no doubt
with its khaki cover, intended for some Tommy's
backpack, a backward solace for off-duty hours
in the trenches: admittedly not very much

on the other hand just the thing I'm talking after;
a talisman perhaps is all, an amulet
with words that say, *buck up, come on, you'll make it,
there's something on after all this,* no matter

what the words say. Housman's "vision," his drear
anguish of love for someone, something, lad
and landscape that never were, that might shoot threads
of gold among the bloody muslins and the mud;

mind wants other news than what the ruffled senses
bring data of—smoke or flesh or birdsong.
It saw there was a space within, reserved
for turning toward another; other; that

no bullet, arrowwood or beach plum might
fill, though these could occupy that space
a moment.
                    Again I heard the casual chirping
of that bird, off in that tupelo, the song

I did not know, below the cries of gull
and jay I did. The unknown I saw was not
enough to satisfy; or—satisfied when it
was framed, complement of what is known for sure.

It's—like—when you go someplace strange, new,
the seashore, any boundary, you want to learn the names
of plants. Start looking at the edges of leaves. It gives
a grip on where you are, and who, or seems to,

to know bullbrier, bearberry, blueberry. You get a GUIDE
or a local to tell. On the dune path I found one, a gnarled
bush alone, hollylike but succulent leaf; nothing
like it in the book. But why feel helped in nature

by a name? When a horde of flower children wanted
to know what they should do to be saved (back when)
Snyder told them, "learn the names of plants;
of animals; learn to do something with your hands."

Well I went out to that dune again: to cop a copy
of the leaf I took and lost: so it's only bayberry
after all; dioecious, two-sexed: some leaves different
from others, that's OK only one got pictured

in my book; but the waxiness, bayberry for sure, set
to be rendered into candles for a *gifte shoppe,*
nauseating noose of "scents." Its nutlets twinkle
near the oily leaves aglow above the sand,

bone white. Doesn't make me feel better to know now
about that scrawny straggler. Sanctimonious
pilgrim know-alls, Bradford & Co.! Forest
into desert, just like that. No time flat, considering.

Triptych

Enameled pocket altarpiece, triptych
with onion-dome brass lunettes, opening to leaves

quartered in panels, each leaf with wing opening
to similarly divided leaves, lunettes. Never

leave home without it! Covered with low reliefs
of His birth; deeds; judgment and suffering;

on the right, four panels show the life and apotheosis
of his mother. In lunettes, the crucifixion, tables

of the law, enthronement of Christ, of Mary, all
on midnight-blue ground sprigged with daubs of white,

chased features of the figures worn down, as are
the engraved legends in Greek above, below.

4 ABOVE THE LAKE

I

Four stories up, the roofscape of slates deepening
from parapet to free-fall space. Slate slick with light,
roofs slid away on every side, off toward the lake
a glacier calved in passing. The sleeping lake—to a boy

it seemed, beyond the elms, the bay of a sea. It was
taboo, that low-railed crow's nest a boy might step from.
Yet sometimes, others napping, unheeded he clambered
out the Palladian window's door, heart tolling loud,

branches roiling; clutched at the scraggy seams
of tar; crawled to the rotting rail that tottered
(what trembled there?); and faced forbidden deeps
of air, cloud, horizon, landlocked waves.

At the elm's lean-to, a few piled clapboards he called
the fort, he hid a ring, his Ring of Saturn;
would turn it, reading the instruction sheet. *You heard
on the radio how the Ring of Saturn helped*

*Buck Rogers save the doctor from the people
on Neptune. That's how valuable it can be!*
It wasn't ribbed like his mother's. Still, Dan had one.
Use it as a secret signal to flash on your pals.

*All you Buck Rogers fans can recognize each other
in the dark with your magic glow rings.* Yes, but what
to do about those Pritchard boys from North Street
who came with acorns, wagonfuls, that really

hurt when they hit him with the pointy ends.
He wondered, puttering in the eddy of days,
Bitty Pritchard and her hullabaloo of foster whelps
holding some meaning for him far aloft

in limbs of an apple, lolling, taking notice.
But an afternoon would come, a moment
beyond the butterflies convening by the mock orange
when he looked at his hands as the continents they were

and he knew the pleasure of their silence,
their final uselessness. Fox into hedgehog, that
was what it came to for him when he saw it clearly,
the likelihood of going inside; a stepping back.

Lupine on hillsides like pinafores, pink and purple,
left on the slopes by girls gone to keep rooms for dust,
to learn a sadness of dentures and walnut dressers.
Another day, up early, riders on blue,

gold, red, pinned to the morning; beyond, the smoldering
bowl of sun caught in cloud; their wheels
turning, Day-Glo Catherine wheels flashing,
dragonfly wings on the white wall of morning—

not thinking, he grasped a nettle in the garden.
They grew there, rooted, undesigned.
His hand, he put his hand in the fire.
He knew the green world, held it close.

2

Long years ago through the unbroken world
he walked an hour, there along the lake
and wooded banks below the shaded houses,
to serve the priest at eight o'clock communion.

A pheasant watched the boy, the boy the bird
where it waited preening before its bushy place;
the boy was on an errand, had an object. Out
on the lake where dawn mist hovered still, the loons

haunted the air with their belonging cries;
addictive, consoling. Far off a car horn seemed
to answer—urge him on. He had begged to go
to serve the Lord and the Rev. Norman Burgomaster,

who asked him to do the eight o'clock. He loved;
and loved the morning, his, before the houses
opened their shades and blinked at him. The Lord
he went to serve might well have been the father,

an English clergyman, for all he knew.
The quest, the steps to the marble altar where
he'd kneel, the justifying pride he took
in wearing the scarlet cassock of St. Andrew

(patron of acolytes) drew him to pour the wine
and water—not the different, scary solace
he felt as crucifer sometimes at later hours.
A rabbit scampered off, plumped down, body

askance by the bridal path eyeing him, the same
boy trudging this way before though now sunshine
and cars were up and whining. But he was seeing
—for he had stared—the eyes intent above him:

the hawk-nosed, gaunt-cheeked visage of him fresh
(or ill) from years among the Inuit; icy
substance the man would embrace, stint of
his Maker, bringing good to Eskimos.

His homilies made his new flock wince, look down;
not wanting elevation, such accent. But the boy
adored that lordly Englishman, judgmental voice
assigning an easy parish its paltry place.

Doors opened and he would see into the light again
but now, how it was all light, not only open spaces
broadcast among crosshatchings of a general scene,
a cloud—had that been dust above the forms of men

in battle? Alarms—a distant scuffle; not only gleams
from breaks in the cloud on swords and pikes; on helmets,
making them look like firemen or football players;
dim spears held high, wavering above the scrimmage

like antennae on huge insect heads, quivering
for data; standards aloft, bright flags; and he
could see through it, survey beyond the fracas; into
the light where all was still; space very deep.

3

He is guarded by Tilopa holding his golden mongoose,
who came to him in Kathmandu; the bronze
White Tara from West Tibet he met on Brattle;
old beggar with his crutch, bone guardian who met him

in D.C.—what kind of bone he wondered; Lha Mo
that Mrs. Bradley brought from China, riding sidesaddle,
keeping her balance, reminding how none gets through alive.
Of course Buddha, Buddha calling the earth to witness;

Buddha, they said from Burma, more likely Nepal,
where in any case Buddha hailed from; here the hunter
with his wallet and dog; and there Bu-dai, hermit
of the marketplace, his bag bursting with dreams

—or money, depending who was talking. And more:
there was an immortal reclining on a cloud
he bought from a missionary, home from a lifetime
with the *heathen Chinee*. The little fellow sound asleep

just might have been transsexual because, although
he wore a beard, someone had bound the feet—
if a cloudy immortal ever was enough a child
for a parent to stunt his feet to stubs. She sported

a bold contented look on her divan of cloud,
a bird sang on her golden crown; the song
looked joyful, but neither was standing watch—though it
was good to dream her company while he slept.

When his father died, one afternoon he found himself
emptying his dresser, the cuff-link drawer,
all those accessories a man once needed. He
could remember daylight coming from a window,

lighting the hour he stole from grieving, sifting
his father's private trove. He had not gone through
that gear since he was eight and found a box
of condoms—got in trouble asking what

the pale balloons were for. Now he could see
his grown-up body in the dressing glass, bending
like a figure musing in a roomscape by Vermeer
although—in his mind's remembering gaze—that day

light came from the right, reversing the source of light
in those old images of calm, of silence glowing.
Cuff links, tie clips, agates his rock-hound father found
and—ground and polished—had set as shirt studs, bolo

clasps, solitaires. Granddad's vest-pocket watch;
and there—a crucifix: or part of it. Only
years later when he'd outgrown St. Andrew's guild
did he learn the man was born and raised R.C.;

it must have been *his* father's, like the watch.
There was the figure of Christ, body of pot metal
(amalgam of dregs, the "mystery meat" of alloys),
a straining body, punctures at hands and feet

for nails to pin it taut. But the cross had vanished;
there was the Lord without those anchoring pins
to hold his attention. Without location, the X
of coordinates, he floundered naked but for swim briefs,

breaststroked among the bright accessories of
a dashing man.
                    Among those tokens, a shard
of amethyst would glimmer at bedside, remedy
prescribed by a gemologist. But his bed

was not the *Pequod*'s deck, St. Elmo's fire
crackling; he no Ahab. No need for Starbuck
to cry *No more witchcraft*, no *God have mercy*
on him grown now, some duties now discharged.

Middens

Wherever spade delves on my acre, shards of other days,
lives, turn up. Nail, crock, dish sliver, bottle, nameless
bone of rust. Six years ago in England I pocketed
a ginkgo leaf I found at Penshurst on the walk,

for Charles—because he spoke of ginkgo leaves
in a poem I liked. Today I found that leaf, unbroken,
dry wafer in a box—stiff miniature olive-green fan.
It wanted to have an odor but had none. I'd never

sent the leaf. Do you know the world is a language
we don't know yet follow bits and phrases of at times?
But then things break, get complicated; you
can't follow the syntax or the words. So desu-ka, Charles?

5 THIRD AVENUE

I

I could stand there, cut it all up, onions, peppers,
tomatoes, romaine and red, the greens, dry them,
tear them up, chop, toss it in a bowl.

Who wants to do all that and then—eat it
alone? Salads are chatty, sociable, so
togetherish at a lamplit table, everyone (or two)

taking helpings. If you're alone, helpings—are
nothing. Better to take bread, a nice sourdough
baguette, bites pulled off; it's a home, private,

a good gnaw in the cave; delicious too,
don't forget that. Ah so, a jug of wine, a loaf
of bread, a green salad beside me in the apartment.

⌒

Drip, drip up the ceiling somewhere, sky touching
skylight whose dome ups the volume to chord with
jets farther aloft, coming in or going out on us,

all of us, the city: a few green aquilegia
still going strong; after cutting back, what's left
of peonies yellowing beside the tub of papyrus,

leaflets brown-tipped; birch and crab leaves falling; soon
none or few along the branches—or, let's say, twigs—
their faint lattice screening vast walls of brick-red

towers thrown up recently, masonry dropping its resolute
pall over rosemary, clematis, chives withering till
about noon, now that sun declines with winter coming.

～

Trees on the skyline twenty stories up, someone's terrace.
Bet they don't have robins (pigeons so adapted they hardly
qualify as wildlife), or squirrels. Somewhere in there

cats are dozing by the hundreds but they don't take to leashes
so on the street it's dogs—today a dog-walker sat resting
on a crate, his dogs standing around, sitting, understanding;

they've all known hours leashed to meters watching in
on their masters at dinner. They look spiffy but hide distress
that shows when they look down, sitting, waiting, confounded

by concrete. Up on the roofs beyond this window, no
nuthatch or jay. Can bees come so far to pollinate
these flowers? Rare the terrace sporting a pat of bird lime.

～

Scrawled note in the lobby: "where was exterminator sign-up sheet
for this month?" I miss squirrels, not rats. Go to the park?
A walk in the park two blocks away at dusk—no squirrels

but a clutch of boys camped in the bushes shouting, "fuck!
OUT of our space!" at the moms and their kids trying to have
picnic supper; daring the moms to come over, screaming

"fuck you you're not the police we have a right to—." Once
they would have carried pails at twilight, leading cattle
to stalls; fishing, or maybe a little recreational

marketing with bow and arrow on the banks of a river;
in the woods, aiming to down a pheasant. "Fuck you!" they hoot
from the shadows by the sign DO NOT FEED THE PIGEONS.

~

You burn daylight sometimes when you're dreaming on
the No. 6 train: *I'm alone in my apartment, then there's
a knock on the door, I peer through the peephole and it's me*

in a silk wrapper. A baby in a stroller beside me, all
eyes; brown eyes eyeing me, the rest of him swathed
in tiny but as yet outsized sweats and sneaks; he's finishing

his bottle eyeing me; Mom, with steady gaze, all "business,"
fifteen or sixteen, holding the bottle, glowing
hair combed back neat. Soon the mother's great black eyes

look down the car, lost—she's still bottle-holding—in thought,
duty, mothering. Last night a black kid—about her age—
sat down across, zoot jeans slung low and cut so full

~

the crotch came to his knees, which yardage with outsize
warm-up jacket enfolded, wrapped him as he hunched, eyes
lowered. Both hands at mouth; I guessed he was mouthing
    something.

Such crossings make a roll, run of scales going off
into the light that falls across them, ordering: when
the rider next to me left, boy lurched over, hands

still at mouth; plumped down, copping quick streetwise
fierce glances my way; kept at it, thumb to the hilt between
lips glistening, fervently reaching like an "Olmec baby"

staring in ecstasy. The infant in the stroller who
broke into my dream is the uneasy inward rider,
and the way the chance-assembled riders swaying together

carefully fail to notice the boy withdrawn into
what pain, intent as they must be on their own
underground going, fleeing wherever they came from to

wherever they go, each body lurching, touching, is
a tone in the arpeggio they make up; at exit they crowd
as one, fit together like the fleshy bracts of

an artichoke. We are forever not letting ourselves
in on our selves, taken up as we are with selves, wrappers,
doubles. Pompous thoughts at 86th Street! Outside

again, on Lex, a flight of pigeons storms down the avenue
in sunlight then, in front of ANNIE'S FRUIT AND VEGETABLES
cuts through to shade; and on, eclipsed; no one the wiser.

2

As a boy Ramakrishna leapt about in trees, amazing
limb-to-limb grace, chattering like a monkey; being
Hanuman, adherent of Rama, attending his god:

Kiran is telling me this as we sit in the White Horse Tavern,
chat over soup and sandwiches. A couple, so close,
at the next table announce they'd be happy—*looks so good*—

to share our meal. They were openly Californian. But we
hold to our space—and talk: he was illiterate. Taught
in parables. Told stories, the Indian way. He was

unstable they say, trances educed by illness; seizures.
Now in a deep samadhi of marble his likeness presides
on the altar of the shrine some Boston ladies built nearby.

. . . See, light in Calcutta comes all at once, the humming stillness
of tropic dawn invades the Great Eastern, high windows wide
for a breath of night air; now day's; kites circling imperious

skies where cloud shreds retreat from ravenous sun.
The city spreads out below fourth-story windows,
everywhere flat-top roofs lie in the muddy light, awash

with sheeted bodies rising, stretching, folding bed cloaks,
waking for the hunt, under alert wheeling of the birds
(this would arouse you, it was somehow that erotic).

Or later at the porch of Ramakrishna's Dakshineswar cell
eyeing the stone where he spent so much time kicking back
in samadhi, and the awful statue of Mother Kali, cruder

than you imagined it. Out in the temple yard a mother—
her babe in arms doing the begging—steers over, his
(remaining) fist shoots out, digits splay, wiggle,

craning for rupees; flies crowd at his eyelids. Stopped
trancelike, excited, you give forgetting you promised the youth
you hired: *no baksheesh.* "Run with me," he cries, pulling you

to the car. Inside, doors locked, daylight canceled by lips,
cheeks, hands, noses flattened, pressed on your glass
bubble. Motionless. Silence. Stop-frame. Six hundred thousand

live on the streets. . . . By midnight bus then, horn and headlight
rouse, divide white-sheeted bodies. As if under water
they rise and part, float in their slo-mo of oblivion.

3

Seferis wrote there was much to be said for the Aegean
but no one had seen it all until he knew the life
on New York subways. (I guess he didn't know that dank

Dakshineswar compound). Two guys get on, one with
bell-bottoms big as skirts, eight rings in each ear (I
count them, he sits beside me), nose ring and lower

lip ring, studs at eyebrows, nostrils; a glittering head
("really loaded" as they say on secondhand lots); his friend
in a Ringling Bros. T-shirt totes a cashmere (or the like)

topcoat now in his lap. They're talking, loud. "A little
reality," the ringed lad says. The other, "it's a little
reality, yeah." —"A little reality." "A little reality . . . "

⌒

Over her body a coat once green hung in strips.
White hair, sharp eye that peered from a face leather
and squinting as one who had spent long months in the trenches;

ankles bruised blue, she wore a man's sneakers (size about
13) like scows on stockingless feet. I stood among
commuters waiting at 42nd Street. She moved in close.

I saw the mahogany welts like badges on her arm
when she reached (all at once she tracked you); dove
into the bin, churn of trash, neatly fished out

the bagged crust of pizza slice I'd just finished
and chucked. Savaged it open; dug in (so much
as gums allowed). Anchorite, shadow rider; twin!

Chink-clang of a trash hauler scooping up the building's
garbage bags—my alarm clock. The truck's tucked my trash
into bed with the stuff of everyone else on the street.

Gnaws sleep wide open—day like a pit toward which
the mudslide of consciousness, prickly with oughtnesses, slides.
List time: this 'n that. Phone! Landlady's dentist. I'm getting

my feet in it, sludge of this blessed day; sun this morning.
Good Godfrey, crows! Crows from nowhere sound their raucous
alarm, chase an intruder back and forth in the canyon

out my window. All I can see is a skein of garment bag
riding an updraft, floating ten stories up, the plastic
silvery in a shaft of light through a rift in apartment towers.

Life on the Mississippi

The gray-blue smoke-roped hairlike light pressing
from fluorescent bars, pressing from the far tin ceiling,
sawdust, drenched floor, squeegee & push broom by wall,
the bar, where the Jibwa sprawled urinating,

awobble, eyes weaving, squaw (as the man says)
squatting, the men, a man standing, feet parted above her
ajar. Satyr brows glaze under light, her blind
stares at them, him, tonight's white trash, the bottom

of snow night on Washington Avenue; no, turn
from look, eye, palm, all hooking at me, grunting
an offer, the cachh of bottle breaking, brown, hard
in a dark hand, the flash and jack shirts folding

over as in a huddle,
separating the two, another
crash, cachh, one body, two
out onto the bench of ice

and two A.M. There at the back, back
of the place, you. I could not
speak. You did not. Eyes
in the smoke. What could I

but climb? Climb,
climb out, back through my days
heart beating a march, the forced
zero march to now-decided dawn.

6   RIDING THERMALS

I

The man had cornered a great deal of money and when it got
hot he went—could go—where it was cool. As for
the servants, well, *tant pis*. A.C. was not yet part
of the picture. But an icehouse. There you had it. The butler's

gopher boy and an upstairs maid called Minnie (whose
lonely duties were smoothing the sheets and emptying
ashtrays) would traipse by separate paths beyond the dairy,
the carriage barn, and slip into an icehouse cool

under pines, closing the door four inches thick behind them
(latch falling to with a clunk) and clinch like godlings, hot
enough to dimple the blocks they lay across, only
a scrim of moistened sawdust clinging to marbly thighs.

Then everything, just so; hospital corners
on a well-made bed. Today, in town, guards barred
the way at a crossing by the racetrack. A single
mount appeared, black flank gleaming in sun

and braided mane all neatly knotted; guided
by an elegant rider in hunt coat, hunt cap, boots
and breeches. Sun shone on velvet cap as they took
their leisurely walk from track to paddock, mob

of autos champing. At twenty paces a dachshund, gleaming
black, gold-collared, brought up the rear of this
procession, little legs atrot, high-stepping—perhaps
low-stepping says it better— oblivious of drivers

not seeing the pet, sounding their horns; who might,
missing the tiny hunter, have run him over.
The dachshund crossed the avenue; inquiringly
looked around. Then crossed once more, returning

trackward, filled with the wan brio of his breeding,
apparently filled with a sense that hereabouts
thoroughbreds come first—before the tourists
in machines, or mothers driving numb to market.

Few have the courage of their metaphors.
But on these afternoons and evenings, loveliness
will not be questioned; will receive a deference
it is due—and need not answer to the press of men.

I was catching up on desk work, writing checks, a few
cards, with my Pilot Precise Rolling Ball, smooth
lines, trusty ballpoint. Stuffed it in my shirt pocket—

I had to get going, get over to Saratoga;
now here I find I left the cap on the butt end.
My shirt is blue, spawning a blue wound over

the left nipple—a lot of never-to-be-written
checks there, congealed in inky fusion above
my heart. Simple forgetfulness? This heat?

I unpacked in a vast bedroom, and pressed the cap
back on. Now, here I am—nothing to spend,
or very little—unreliable me

and my empty cartridge, disposable duo.
I glimpsed dear Cole as he was leaving; he
fled without good-byes. Five years ago

we met and talked at breakfast half an hour.
He didn't say good-bye. He never did
good-byes. Back then, he was a guest in the room

where I am now the guest. My friend, the wicker
chair is looking at me now, where Howard,
May, and Sylvia seemed to be watching you.

Talk about the mighty dead! And now
your spirit too, lugging your big-boned frame,
looks on. We are each lonely, have known betrayal.

2

Still have stiffies, don't you? a new friend asked
walking through a shower to Southwoods
for drinks. That's putting it to you

a voice in the ear's mind was hinting.
Bravely I offered: they say now don't they
the self's discovered topside, not

belowdecks? Who you are is who you
get along with thinking you are; you
are determined in your brain—the man

on the box is so, well, reassuring. —Damn,
one is not one's balls although
it does help to have them along—or (these days

ᵔ

technicians say) identity need not reside in this
headline-grabbing polluted dumpsite,
hot ticket for sound bites this year,

not every guy's personal Love Canal
but all the instruments agree it is for more
than a few. Know what I'm saying? It's all

the rage. But just you wait; it's the seat
of something central you find out one day
when doctors from the body's EPA

have cleaned it up and hosed it down
and cut you loose.
The old fantasy life—how strange to find it so

ᵔ

distinct, discrete—that dream world too—like
an apple with a huge bite chomped from it;
old yens become old yens, not much more

absent as leaves from the trees come winter solstice.
*The time you may in me behold when yellow
leaves, or none, or few. . . .* So what this double

thing proposes, brain disposes? Sadness—
for the little things that made him briefly glad—
nought proposed, airy nothing disposed;

I can remember memories, they go like stories
written by others. Those moments past: were they
the work permit assigned to me, the hod

of the hod carrier, the hoe of the laborer
in his field, the staff that comforts him at rest
when the sower comes along the furrow casting?

What made me think I was a man? How so?
This is the life. Boy, has the world I lived in
fooled me good! The whole thing now we're told

is nothing. *We can fix it.* Goodness,
the ads for miracles, some dusky gleeful
couple in the gushing twilight of their years,

sheepish, transfigured by passion, like Titania
and Bottom on her bed of flowers. You say
the mind has other fish to fry. Without a pan?

3

To love or not to love is all the legend on the card
that Gregory sends, an English postcard, NOT
FOR SALE—and why not I wonder, or does

this epistolary freebie, this giving of the old
either/or canard, have something sly to do
with charity? In this town where the animal is king,

what about that animal love a writer friend
has a man in her story recommend as just the thing
when he attempts to seduce a woman

during dinner; and then, what might animal love
after all, in the event, be? I do not know. Lust
perhaps, but is that meant, a rutting woodchuck

with one eye on the oval of light, its avenue
of escape, should threat threaten from
even farther down its warren of tunnels, its

earthen hole? Jon told of a big dog dish
loaded with dog food on a porch in Wyoming
raccoons scoped out; plenty of room for three

to sup but each could hardly get a mouthful in
edgewise for its coon's requirement to bite
its fellow coons, an animal's vicious circle of

aggression against its kind. Sex is forever fun
but not fun forever; does not give in to the odor
of eternity, that great white ring of endless

light. Oh, no; I do think not. Writers in their
stories, which are fictions after all, say so
perhaps because they do not find much else

to write about, do they, a certain feeling of
quiet desperation as to subject matter, animal
love plug-able in-able? There's a market for it

the way in 1800 there was a market for sublime
descriptions of landscape combined with swooning
yet priggish feelings, breathings of women in a state

of girlitude. Now, there's always, for example,
the skunk problem in Provincetown, the skunk
protected species we can't protect ourselves from

and have to call the outlaw skunk man, $35
a head, instead of going through legally appointed
guardians of skunk, Peaceable Kingdom Lawmen

who charge $150 per head; and where
do they take the skunks later, on that frail
arm of sand flexing out into the Atlantic?

Out to the Beech Forest or the dune shacks?
Skunks eye a house like woodchucks, possible
residence for a clan with a litter of kits.

There's animal love, aromatherapy
on the hoof—or in the claw—breeding cute
beasties that are no friend to man

or woman. I could tell you about the time a mother
and her young adopted our garage—the door
didn't work. We left them to a Texan lad with a .22

who had experience of pests attacking in armor:
armadillos needing more firepower than a .22,
animal-cleansing near El Paso. Which

comes first in these latter days of environment
law, the house for US or the
animal? Let's all roll together and cry out

in anguish like the squirrel, one gray thew with
boa tail, hurling itself side to side in animal
terror at the Havahart trap controlling it.

Brutal—slugging it out with heat; I feel like
Hansel in the oven, soon to be weather's snack food
in a wet T-shirt, holding on like a terrier at a hole

to this page rumply as Kleenex in these billows.
A gasp of air—can't call it a breath—and a shade
whaps up, WHACKS the ceiling, falls back

letting a flash of sky in; the heat's breaking
the sky; presses down with a leaden full nelson.
I barely walk to the machine as thunder

drums, rolls of far-off warning
muffled in mist muslins; sharp
wires of lightning short-out first one

window then another; heat lightning; SILENCE.
I bend to the machine, turn off, unplug,
disconnect from the storm that cancels light

and streams down aslant. Soak up a puddle
with a bath mat: on the sopping chartreuse
a long dead insect flattened dry in profile

just like a fossil, legs curled long ago
in a little row, fixed in limestone.
Pressure of heat dies off as the rain

heads east. Weak lightning arcs fizzle from
cloud to ground beyond the pines. The crows
hightailed it out of here or lurk at their posts

waiting among high branches. Swifts
and robins test the fresh calm of air,
from drenched, slow-nodding spruces, glide

low to the ground as if keeping safe
distance from the weather up there, cloud
cover gone dangerous. Two or three at a time

reconnoiter over the stunned field; go off
on their timeless errands. I'm just
as lucky as a bird—but thinking about it:

like a man reaching shore in a storm
no longer drowning, lying there in the
stones and bladder wrack and pools

thinking, *hey, you made it*. You get
used to dying and it isn't cruel; suddenly
here's another chance and *it* isn't cruel

either. Heat's off. Low pressure gone.
What goes around comes around. It's
a heady moil of cyclicals but when

you're in a trough there is *not* crest; when
you're down no up could be. —What
were you going to say? And how? You toil not

but O, don't you wish for hard labor? "Life"
whatever on earth that means comes along,
intervenes. Should you pray? Pray for

salience of pain to make your instance clear
and present, or accept what comes—however
sweet—and burst joy's Granny Smith? You bet.

The blank page at morning is nothing compared
to the blank eye content to look at deep sky
where not a bird or cloud plumbs the depth

and no one knows what's up, how much is left.
But this is really different here, let's say; stretch out
those muscles & tendons (ouch!) on the front side

of the shoulder, back, rib cage—sore neglected,
tired, weak. Massage those fascia, ball of bone
crackle in socket; rub down with an oaken towel!

Talk about lethargy: when it's this
muggy, talk about lethargy is too much work.

I am looking at one butterfly left after so many
Monarchs and Admirals got done in by that pesticide

virus. There! it flutters along the canyon
of hemlocks but has no squadron, no wing group; it wanders

solo, only hunting and gathering left, no larking
left to do; alone, a chance survivor; all

the other wing-pairs it took to lift a quorum
missing, missing in action—from action. I

seem to be running along like this one; heat
irons me flat on the floor, a little snooze

while it may not seem in order is a foregone
necessity and off I go into dreamless—or

apparently dreamless—nap, pastures new, storing up
enough cud to enable me to get up and do

what has to be done, for example laundry or
bookending my work projects with those bookends

I saw depicting Poe, all spiffy and stern
like Beethoven in stock collar and tailored jacket.

What would it mean to me or to that entourage
of my close associates, lost among hemlocks or

somewhere out West staggering under the burden
of an insect disease, if I pulled off some lyrics like

"Ulalume" or "Annabel Lee" and published them
in *Graham's Magazine* or some ladies' annual

to the great acclaim of practically, well, nobody
I knew anything about, but a reception so wide

and Eliotic in reverence that it would seem quite
superfluous ever to write anything again

resting on those laurels I confidently knew
were there and deserved—or thinking about the strength

in depth my kind of butterflies after all had; huge
clouds of them painting some absent landscape bright

hues—though one, here, alone, casting about among
the hemlocks, appears to be looking for a flower;

appears to be solitary, the only example of a kind;
a *one-off* beauty whose unique if slight and lonely

manifestation of the infinite creativity of its maker,
or evolution's cook, clearly indicates the presence

somewhere of an agency so vigorous, a population
so ample and industrious, that all the poems in the world

might be perfected under the guidance and tears of
this great cloud of unknowing, of creatures

of the most evanescent yet inspired order
whose vigor pollinated and reclaimed the flora

of an entire world, permitting it to go on
into a massive, fertile, unplanned future

teeming with seedlings, insects, oxygen, offering
shade, ports for nests, fruit, delightful

vistas and green thoughts for a populace
of poets and their affectionate stalwart dear

readers working hard at their work, professions,
their day jobs, and curling up come night without

the tube, with sheaves of poems of all the poets
of the world, knowing that health and strength, and some

final pleasure were to be found in poems
and being found there fashioned into

sustenance—love out of strength, ease
out of health, and out of pleasure, assurance; and more.

The butterfly is fading; zigzagging off, but
rain or frost will down him, lightweight

drifter riding the thermals, days mapped out
by either chance or instinct, maybe a quick

flyby of a supermarket (but keeping faith,
keeping blinders on in the aisles): dire

basics is all we can ever afford, knowing we'll
crash by nightfall or buy the farm tomorrow. Still

holding his own, though—look! that's him, old Dr.
Hope, leaning over real close and listening to

the strings of his guitar after he's stopped
strumming! There's Hope for you, if that's who it is.

Codger

"Get away," cried the man, "get away!" The one over there
by the tree, the man with a big heart, giving each kid
a necklace of tears. He says, "I'm seventy-nine

I never smoked like all these whippersnappers
smoking at twenty like old stoves, wait
till they get to be my age, JUST WAIT. Doctor says to me

now just hang in there Fred. I said what else can I DO
I'm not suicidal so I'll just have to, won't I? But
those young fellas, let them have their fun."

And the young ones turn, running to endless arbors,
endless as far as they can tell, where grapes
swell and newts climb among rotting melons.

7 ANTIPODES

I

Ah, the secret ministry of camping gear
that shall cover the bodies of the young
in storms and cold of night; feed them in achy

mornings of frost on the cold camping ground!
You walk exhausted reaches of Second Avenue
where buses envelop the little shops in haze,

consider Edenic forays at the Salvation Army's
window: sleeping bags bright with brand names, a pup tent,
crampons already hinged to pre-owned boots,

mix with an ancient Magnavox, someone's
fox fur wrap, and a willowware tureen.
Among these wearables and ornaments

☞

a *Webster's Unabridged,* and you can see—at five
dollars—the cheapest item in the window. Talk
is cheap was a saw that came to mind lugging

the thing back home—and words are heavy. . . . It's
what you do on your time off, trekking, writing,
that counts . . . adds up to. . . . Dusk is beginning to fill

the street and damn if you aren't mooning again
as shops clang shut, ringing their corrugated
curtains down, closing their grates across

windows. You're thinking again how easy to be
alone and focused in the city where millions
go about minding their business, and you think

how nice because you know they're doing what
they have to do, where in the hills and the necky towns
everyone is keeping track; anonymity is just

a concept from Outer Space. In city pent,
you know what you want; "dilution," then dissolution
of desire; shaky succor of unregard,

solace of withdrawal, refuge inexpressible,
lamplighter slowly unweaving the haze along
a darkening street. A siren fading down

the street just now, and cries of joy then laughter
from the sports bar on the corner; suddenly
just now is gone; and you are recalling how

you went fishing with the boy—avid, his lovely
scrawn, determined, patiently ignorant of
origin or outcome of this play, that sport

with dark water at dawn, miracle of body-
contact with untouched air. How can I hope
to say, fear palpable, what is; murmurs

on the air still inarticulate in me. How
would he answer; might he answer if with luck
I spoke well—or well enough? But what's to say now,

his sister gone to an island in an ocean the other
side of earth; or him, my opposite number? Ah,
farewell, you two; voyagers, fare forward!

2

Their mother called from downstairs, *are you all right?*
I answered, crashing, *happy as a pig in shit.*
The boy is listening and he calls, *what's*

he doing? She relays upstairs, *what are you doing?*
—*Lying on my bed,* I answer. He shouts, *great name*
for a band! Now which remark is he thinking of?

I wonder, dozing off. But only for a minute.
Bang and thud, the boy is setting up
in the living room, guitar, the amp, the speaker,

wah-wah pedal, makings for the great litter,
enough loud sound to wipe the neighborhood
of what-we-hear when everything's turned off.

He plans to sell the half-stack Marshall speakers
to Patrick from Schenectady if Patrick can discover
how to drive up here through snow this afternoon.

What massive things it took to make them glad!
Panzer divisions making preemptive strikes
into a hapless calm, defenseless homes;

their annexation of grownups' *lebensraum.* . . .
          And now like an animal in spring losing
his winter coat, my son is shedding another

protective layer; amp and all is going, he
is building capital to buy a car, to gain
cross-country highways. Home is where you leave from

and soon he'll be on his way to all the space
he is a part of, to learn by occupying,
as before with loudness, now with distance,

where he lived and how, that street he knew
like the palm of his hand, off in a corner of green
up-country hills. Directly south of here we saw

a sign on the interstate that read, *highest
elevation till Oacoma, South Dakota.* What
could it mean? Flatlands are long; he can't know how long,

who knows the bud of growing rooted in one spot.
No snap, these miles he's staking out to go
before he sleeps the sleep of one who knows.

3

Litter, I wonder what that might be, the stuff of
a cosmos with radius of fifteen billion light years—or
a gaggle of puppies adorable on wall-to-wall

broadloom? Look at the stars. We want to know
if there's order, structure in matter, somehow find out
if clumping's going on, dumpiness however slight

out there, or if it's all randomness that evens out
when we get enough distance to view it from,
flattens out into a uniformity like

a linoleum pattern of sprayed dots; or stars.
I want to consider appropriation, jet travel,
the travel that takes us into it; Hemingway in

Kenya or Schneebaum in Irian Jaya; small-scale
societies in the middle of large-scale structures; how
can one of us—Americanos—possibly

presume to comprehend the sleepy anguish
in a populace like Morondava's or Lake Sentani's,
who'd rather not survive on rice or sago and yams.

The woman needs to sell her woven basket
for a cotton print, the man who carves ancestors
for market envies cannibal tourists who pay;

and pay to see where they are told it was
that missionaries and their ilk got boiled for dinner.
This evenness of things on itty-bitty Earth's

large scale—at odds with that unevenness of things
on smaller scales. For I consider the awesome
abyss of galaxies, the unhomogenizing fracas

of deep space, the peaceful river of the Milky Way
or unimaginable girth of superclusters, great
walls of fire, crash of surf booming at swimmers

on our shifting shores, a sound dubbed *pink* by these
cosmologists divining what is there, then kenning
way beyond. I must take particles into account now,

exotic bits such as neutrinos, all the matters
that matter when I try to "contextualize"—awful
surmise—myself in eternity that great white—

pink!—ring of endless light. It's a little . . . much.
I'll keep to the basics then, like what are we doing here
on this street corner of the system for a millisecond

then *pfft*. The only thing we *can* do is—
learn more about it.
                              My son, you said you wished
we didn't have bodies. Flesh is drag weight, sure,

but that changes as you grow. Fun—for a while.
Metaphysical existence would perchance be less
problematical, wouldn't it! But we, we are

embodied; so.
                    . . . So it's important to know
my blood type—vaguely I recall *A positive*—
if I'm going to have surgery (the surgeon had

a cancellation and fit me in). But we don't know
your type, and we're not sure of mine. No way
to get two pints for backup; the local hospital

won't do the trick, Red Cross the only folks
statewide who draw donations—but come downstate
just once a month. No way my son, or I, can be

my donor. So it was iffy but I went along
under the blade without the backup.
                                              I sit now
on the back porch watching crows sashay on grass.

They look remarkably hot in their full black coats,
they keep in the shade under the hemlocks and old
arborvitaes; work regardless of other birds

if other birds stay out of their way. Hunt
and peck, hunt and peck and make a ruckus
if foreigners scout their turf. Yet they and their

bossy ways will fall silent, vanish, their glade
forgotten; and none to do the forgetting as the planet
careens onward another billion years.

Stuff to ponder. Yet thinking about all that,
it's irrelevant. I might have, one chance in thousands,
contracted hepatitis B or C—or worse.

When I consider my place off here—in the galaxy
I see the other rim of when I look up
at the Milky Way—I see the odds of "thousands"

look fairly—well, really quite—high, a mere
passel compared to winning a lottery or
the cluster of galaxies my galaxy is sitting in,

10 to the 7th power light-years wide. How cliché
to acknowledge being infinitesimal in
a system that, in its own way, is infinitesimal!

Can't do it; nor can you. Out the window I watch
a hummingbird at the cleome. We're father and son.
Our doom is love.
                        . . . Today I left the nozzle of the hose

attached to the faucet draped over the rim of my
claw-footed tub: the faucet has a microscopic
leak, *drip drip,* and soon—that is, after five hours—

the drops began to drip from the ceiling into
the room below; mea culpa, yes; *I've seen
a lot worse* quoth the night man, and the super

next morning amazingly said, *things happen, people
live in that building say three Hail Marys, heh,
go back to work.*
                              I start by reading; can't imagine

what problems a genius like Gödel might dream
and solve (his mathematical systems—hence mine—
he showed, were incomplete. Not all that's true,

he proved, can be proven to be true). So.
Gödel proved that? The little mystic! And yet
that's highly comforting. If we had not

physical existence, might we be even less
reliable, predictable? I do not matter
in the great scheme of matter, but job one

is still to figure out how I fit in or might,
if it should come to pass that I had after all
a niche waiting, some bower of answers ripe for picking

in a supercluster far away. Darned if the stars
aren't there even when it's cloudy! We're sure of that;
even when fireworks left over from the Fourth

at the track go up on the 14th in a blaze,
light and white noise, the guys defining their kicks
without a thought for the siren bearing down

on the fun, the clamor; and the starscape facing
the other way just out there, disregarded
by grooms and muckers, stable hands, apprentice jockeys,

a stray owner fretting late over a yearling
he hopes to auction off to an Arab for serious
cash. Learning makes sense; "try ignorance," as

the bumper sticker says, and here he is, my son
going off; away to a life; no car this time
but a plane, the 747 burning off ten tons

of kerosene each hour, littering the sky;
belting out that heat into the atmosphere,
velocity getting everyone where they want to get.

Lobster Cove

A swan along the sun-glare of the tide leads on
his mate, following yards behind. At the head
of Lobster Cove, moves close to the granite wall,
turning his glowing crimson beak to cast

an eye on the man who watches there. Light
reflecting off water flashes at the stainless white
of swan—and glares around him. Tip of beak
backlit by sun, like molten iron just

from a furnace. Seeming to yearn, the beak tucks back
in a frieze of feathers; one eye—like Daphne straining
to look from the tree of herself—peers from otherness
at our life; black eye staring, piercing, steady.

8 BUZBY AFTERNOON

I

By turns the light went oily yellow, then slate,
then olive; it seemed to look in windows at you

then turn away. A presence rose as if
a great breath was taken and lungs strained

to fill, and the chest rose out. You go around
unplugging, turning off, heaving to, as if

"folding your tents to silently steal away"
and think, it is a stillness wiped clean—the house

BUCKED then, grandest sires among the trees
fell, deadweight, free, both fore and aft of us

a scissor-lock for sure, a branch still wearing
foliage waved, Magritte-like, from a bedroom ceiling.

I am avoiding stress, we all should, it's good
for everything around us; but here it was, God

or the weather, the wholly Other coming along
signifying its will through, well, the weather;

WAS the weather; or manifests itself at any rate
thusly. Here it was, I was feeling it, lightning—white

in tooth and claw. Tornado, turn me, selah!
Don't let enemies breach the gates. Find champions

to defend and hold. Put out the wind; wrench
that hovers, take off from me. The abyss opened—

and shut—like twin leaves of a cellar door falling
to granite plate, locking wind out, dark in.

A man crept through tree limbs ambushing the front door,
slipped in. Slickered, but still drenched when he shed it.

He was a big man, young, and frightened; and wore
a CD cap. Said he was lost, could he come in.

You're in already, I said, happy to have a guest.
He warmed himself at kitchen candles. Couldn't stop,

"damn, that's a big ole boy. Oh, Lord." He'd fall
silent, gaze at the candles, then: "good gracious,

Almighty!" He suited up; had to get home. I
asked where he lived, a host's ancient privilege.

He went back out into gale-force wind saying,
"O Mighty! I just live the next street over."

Too much to handle then, I didn't take it in,
what happened out. A spruce branch, huge, by the sprung

trunk of a sugar maple; how did it get there, on
what gale—the spruce trunk still standing? I climbed the stairs

and looked on high, it was the tip, a nudity
topside, we'd been spruce-lopped. Birds didn't know

where to perch; in a day—without their maple canopy—
sun blanched the elephant magnolia leaves. Everything

salaamed eastward, ligularia, bee balm, even
the stocky hostas lay flat so their white ankles

showed; like a full square of the faithful outside
a mosque when the muezzin calls them to prayer.

. . . Lilies lay down on the prayer rug of the grass. . . .

A sunny morning at last and I don't have to
worry about the bad stuff—tornado drearies

and young fogies penning ambitious hearts out
down in town; I can do dress-ups and church.

Why I do it I'll never know but at least
it's not to listen to the deacon's sermon. There's always

the cosy threat of a nice garage sale driving home,
but really I'm not into possessions anymore

especially since the Lord, or Krishna, the voice
(however it's called this time) out of the whirlwind

did a job on my ancient maples—in about five seconds—
and my house *bounced* when the trunks fell, back and front.

Celebration for "Sophie Our Deacon" on her first
decade in the Deaconate. She used to be

"one of the guys, and drank 346 Rum,"
said Don from his crutches remembering other days

and then he's presenting her with a "communion kit,"
chalice and paten (there must be a tonier word

for that box of ritual silver implements;
sounds like they're giving her a sacrament set

to take camping). Sophie talks about her call,
St. Francis was her idol in those days when,

renouncing her old life, she'd seen the light.
Studying the new, she'd read *this biography*

on St. Francis—"he hated those lepers, though,
and couldn't bear to touch them. He had taken

a vow of poverty, which pretty well
meant taking up the cross of selflessness.

Well, one day he met this leper on the road
and he just went for it, embraced him, then

kissed him on the mouth! At which the face
bulbous and dark as corn smut vanished and—

was Christ." That was the way she felt in this
parish, this town where she'd grown up, "easy,

so easy, living like him with friends, a family,
ministering to them like Francis with the leper."

2

Another summer: brook behind the inn, a tiny
wetland spilling grass, lime-green water, default

of current making it pond, radiant with slime
flowing or still by uncut lawn. Two boys

age five or six holler in jockey briefs, their stringy
bodies freed from proper breeches ages back,

mud feet, legs, smeared arms, smeared faces—delicious;
jockeys mud-hued—with a hint of lime—someone's

German shepherd barks, prancing, splashes, running
off then back and sloshing in, mud-tykes and dog

loud, sliming joy's grape, plenum of pleasure
jumping, reaching in then out of goo, arms wheeling,

fingers splayed in delight, abandon, speed: the
shouts and laughter, their little blessedness. We

watch them, touching, from an arbor on the bank
that leans—like the waterlogged plank bridge below

half sunk in the stream it crosses—their muddy beaming
faces, life unconscious of anything on earth

but concord with dirt—freedom in the lime moment
of twilight; for the sun's dropped behind the hill. Shade

sweeps the green beyond the inn, where once twelve inns were,
an empty square now. A light goes on, lights up

a gas pump; another, the spine of the meetinghouse,
doors locked below an elaborate Palladian window.

3

Driest Vermont summer in one hundred seven
years, leaching

ajuga and nettles out of the dead
garden; last year's

tornado took our fifteen trees down; all
those haywire shrubs:

hedgerow honeysuckle, mock orange, coiled
screen of creeper.

A lone walnut lopped naked, a few twigs
with leaves sprouting.

Logs, once grown trees squeezed by python cables
of bittersweet

~

looking now like those spiraling pillars of the
baldachino

in St. Peter's, yet holding, here, nothing up;
good stuff gone,

backhoed, getting downed trees out. Now,
clear views of

garbage, car batteries long dead, stacked behind
a neighbor's garage,

hidden only from their owner; smashed kiddy
pools blue and pink;

surplus Baptist popcorn dumped after church
Sunday nights.

~

The reverend minister behind the garden has
gone off on a toot or the family vacation—

loaded up the old Volvo wagon and off
they've gone without their choir—leaving behind

Tom Hill the siding man who's sawing
metal, strips painted white, and nailing them

onto the sides of the parsonage and here
and there to the church spire or at least

doing something helpful to the belfry
in a constructive way so that the electric

cross has had to come down and now
it lies there on the grass like a wired pair

of discarded railway ties. It's all all right,
I can listen to the neighborhood in summer

sprucing up: and so can the Scotty next door,
boorish terrier very involved in this

renovation, loudly in denial or disapproval
of the noise, sounds of hammering, clatter of

metal ladder getting moved, and aluminum
getting cut to size on sawhorses with a

randomly screaming portable circular saw.
Buzby is riled, his sentry instincts up

and going, alert and yipping loud as he can,
running to and to and fro and fro;

hasn't been inside all afternoon. When my
teen got home from a hot day at work,

Buzby wanted that explained, likewise.
So the boy doesn't want that music to relax to

and turns on his guitar, the amp, the speakers,
going at it, vibrating over to Buzby, smoothing

everything out, and I guess Mr. Tom the siding man
is listening; or's gotten lulled into slowing

down on his hammer, the cut straps whapping
a little in the breeze as they get lifted up

to the parsonage bedroom walls. The afternoon
goes into tone-poem mode, and now my Oriental

lilies are going at it without a sound:
opening, blooming, wafting their musky

honeyed perfumes; engulfing the grass, the hedge;
over the fence, getting over to Buzby, getting—

or, as may be, not getting—to the siding man
as shadows move silently toward the lilies, a dusty

pollenish gray or—as they might have found it
in the stop-frame quiet of yards in an earlier age,

maybe 1939—purple, redolent
like a cut-glass scent bottle all but empty thrown

on a refuse heap, its bevels catching rays
of sun beside the rinds of orange halves.